The Ramblings of the Man Who Isn't Very Good at Making Beds

JAMES WEBB

Copyright © 2018 James Webb

Cover photograph copyright © 2018 Mark Lewis

The contents of this book have appeared previously in weekly
portions as James's Blog at www.thelisteningbook.org.uk

All rights reserved.

ISBN: 1-9997464-4-9
ISBN-13: 978-1-9997464-4-5

CONTENTS

Introduction 1
The Small Things 3
(Mis)Understanding Parables 5
Exchanging the Truth of God For a Lie 9
When Perfection is the Enemy of Good 15
Gath and Adullam 17
Reasons to be Cheerful 19
Some Beautiful Waste 23
Dude, Where's My Peace? 25
No Blog Post This Week 27
My Wife 29
Hide & Seek with God 31
What's a Father to Do? 33
And Lead us not into Temptation, but Deliver us from Evil 35
Anyone for Seconds? 39
Based on a True Story 45
The Stone and the Seed 53
Outsmarted 57
As One with Authority 61
Love is not Fair 65
Another Lost Argument 69
The Music of Easter 73
Upside Down Food 75

"Peace Be With You" 77
Throw Away Encouragements 81
Five Random Thoughts on the Subject of Trusting God 83
Psalm 139 for the Modern Pulpit 85
A King of Two Halves 89
Five More Thoughts on the Subject of Trusting God 93
Fellow Pilgrims 97
Noises that Sound Good 101
The God of All Comfort 105
Skimming the Sun 107
One Trick Pony 109
The Best Defence is a Good… Silence? 111
Father's Day 113
Meta Edition 117
McChurch 121
Empty Hands 123
More Daily Bread Thinking 125
In Memory of Dick Vesey 127
Lost in Translation 129
For the Quiet Ones 133
Bad Examples 135
It's True 137

Talking About Yourself 139
Memory Lane 143
Seven Thoughts for Preachers 147
Alone in the Dark 149
The Wind and the Waves 151
A Week in the Life of... 153
Cold-Calling... 155
Three Years a Blogger 159
About the Author 161
Books by the Same Author 163
More Posts 167

JAMES WEBB

INTRODUCTION

What do we say when we bump into a friend? Probably things like "Hello, how are you?" or "What's been happening?" That's all well and good, but over the years I've been asked some different questions, and have added them to my arsenal. Questions like "What's God been doing in your life?" or "What has God been saying to you recently?" Questions that assume that God is both real and active in our lives, on a daily basis and in the most mundane things.

These are questions I save up for Christians, but some of the responses I've received would have made Richard Dawkins proud. Asking one of these questions is sometimes like lobbing a grenade into a conversation.

The point is, for some of us who follow Jesus, the idea that God is doing something in our life, or might have something to say to us, is a totally foreign concept. One that has never occurred to us, and if it has, it's certainly never been something that we think that we can talk about in non-Sunday conversation.

My blog has tried to serve two purposes over the years. I try to write as though someone has asked me, "What has God been doing or saying recently?" and I hope that what I write inspires my readers to ask that same question of themselves. In short, I hope that my blog posts are both questions *and* answers.

So bear that in mind when you make your way through this book. Ideally, each entry reveals something that I believe God has said to me, and ideally it challenges you to think about what God has been saying to you.

Because He is saying something, you know.

The Small Things

02 November 2017

I'm not an adventurous person, but the twists and turns of my life suggest that, for me at least, God implements such things as 'compulsory adventures'. The problem is that being between adventures leaves me tormented by restlessness. I'm not exaggerating for effect (who me?). 'Tormented' is a carefully chosen word. I suspect this is a condition I'll have to deal with for the rest of my days. It's difficult.

My mistake is to think that life is about these big, momentous experiences, and eavesdropping on our culture only reinforces this misunderstanding. As a rule, we're encouraged to sleepwalk our way through the week, looking forward to the weekend, or a holiday, or the Next Big Thing. It's true that life can feel like long periods of boredom punctuated by brief periods of excitement, but only being enthusiastic about adventure is no way to live.

Actually, those long periods of boredom are crucially important. It's the small things that we fill our lives with that make the difference, and as Richard Wurmbrand said, "Saints are those who do small things well." The fruit of our lives comes from what we plant in the uneventful, not what we do on our compulsory adventures. We think that significant Christian leaders, the sort of people whose stories are told long after they are gone, are significant purely because they make the most of big opportunities. No. They're men and women who make the most of the small things, and when the big things come their way they're already so used to putting God front and centre that they take advantage of adventures out of habit. If you keep God to one side, waiting for something big to come along, then you'll find that He won't fit into your life because you've already filled it with junk.

Today's blog post is just for me. I need to remind myself of what is true, especially during these grumpy weeks. Sitting down, staring in front of a blank screen and painfully squeezing words onto a page is good medicine. It's one of the small things that I need to fill my life with in order to qualify for the next compulsory adventure.

(Mis)Understanding Parables

09 November 2017

I don't normally divulge the meaning behind the stories that I've written, partly because I don't want to prejudice the reader and partly because I'm a contrary so-and-so, but let's talk about the story 'Border Control'. This one appears in *The Second Listening Book* and, as usual, I had something deliberate in mind when I wrote it. I believe that the Gospel changes our fundamental character; not tidies it up, or papers over it, but actually transforms it. We were sinners, we are now children of God. However, some Christian leaders undermine God's grace by teaching that we should continue to define ourselves by our old nature – as though the Gospel is some kind of illusory magic trick that makes us look good to God but offers no real change. I tried to express my frustration with this bad theology through 'Border Control', a story set at an immigration station, where the guards funnel new arrivals into a holding camp and leave them thinking that being trapped behind barbed wire is the same as being a free citizen of their new country.

I wrote it before Brexit and President Trump made immigration into an even more divisive topic, but the story has only been available since those events. One reviewer took the parable at face value, assumed it was liberal political commentary on immigration and took me to task on my naïvety. Now, I am naïve, but only because I'm consistently surprised when people don't get what I'm really trying to say. You'd think I'd have learned by now.

Someone else once commented that they didn't get one of my parables, and that this made it a bad parable, because the meaning of parables are supposed to be clear. Unsurprisingly, I disagree. The disciples, who knew Jesus best, floundered repeatedly on this issue, scratching their heads and saying, "Tell us what this parable means…" once the crowds had dispersed. When they summoned up the courage to ask Jesus why he used parables in the first place, Jesus responds by quoting Isaiah: "You will be ever hearing but never understanding; you will be ever seeing but never perceiving."

I don't mind people not understanding my stories and I don't mind them getting something other than what I originally intended – that's actually quite exciting. What I do mind though is people thinking that I'm a one-dimensional writer. It's OK for me to get my ego bruised once in a while, but it's also OK to come away from a parable confused, or encouraged, or feeling like you've been kicked in the gut.

Thanks to two thousand years of Sunday School, we think we 'get' parables, but let's be honest. Had we been there when Jesus first spoke, we likely would have missed the point too. If Jesus turned up today in Hyde Park and told the parable of the Prodigal Son for the first time I'm sure that there would be some Evangelicals lining up to lambaste him for being soft on sin. If he'd told the parable of the Workers in the Vineyard I'm sure that sections of the American Religious Right would have denounced him as a 'dangerous socialist'. It's almost like Jesus was looking for trouble, using stories that arouse confusion and anger in equal measure.

Everyone these days knows that Samaritans are Good, but when Jesus first told that parable, Samaritans were anything but. 'Samaritan' was a crude swearword that a good Jew, a Jew like the one who asked Jesus the original question in Luke 10, couldn't even bring himself to say. There are plenty of despised people groups at the moment. Think of the one group that makes you the most suspicious; the ones that you find it the easiest to hate and the hardest to love. Would you have followed Jesus if he'd recast one of them as the Samaritan in his parable?

The thing is, it was people like us – people with opinions – who wanted Jesus dead.

Exchanging the Truth of God For a Lie

16 November 2017

It always begins with a lie. In the garden, the first of us chose to reject the truth, and chose to believe a lie. It broke us; sold us into slavery. Ever since the first, the Father of Lies has been keeping us in our chains by sidling up to us, and in a pleasant tone of voice asking what seems a most reasonable question: "Did God really say…?"

"Did God really say that He would be with you, whatever you face? If that's the truth, then why do you feel so alone?"

"Did God really say that you are worth something to Him? If that's the truth, why do your failures define you?"

"Did God really say that following Him brings life to the full? If that's the truth, why are you so bored and disillusioned?"

The lie seems to make sense of our experience, so we believe it.

But does the lie make sense of our experience, or does our experience just confirm that we have already believed the lie?

Is God really absent, or do we just *believe* that He is absent? Are we really defined by our failures, or do we just *believe* that we are defined by our failures? Is this really as good as following Christ gets, or do we just *believe* that this is as good as following Christ gets?

You know the stuff that Jesus says? What if it were true? All of it? What if the problem is not that it's false, but that we don't believe it? What if "God really *did* say…" and the only reason we don't enjoy the freedom of this truth is because we choose the chains of a lie instead.

Why would we do that? Why would anyone choose to believe what is not true?

I don't know why we do, but we do. Perhaps it's because by the time we encounter the truth, we are already weighed down by a thousand lies. Perhaps it's because it really does seem too good to be true. Perhaps it's because we just don't know the truth as well as we think that we do. Perhaps it's because trusting God is just too much of a risk for us right now.

A lie is something false, but if you believe it then you give it power. What is unreal becomes real, and it controls the way that we relate to the world.

Don't believe me?

There was once a man whose car suffered a flat tyre whilst driving along a deserted country road. He had a spare, but was unable to change it because, when he went to look, his jack was missing. What to do?

Looking into the paddock on his left, he noticed – far in the distance – a building. It must be a farmhouse, he reasoned, and hopping over the fence he began walking, hoping that the farmer would have a jack that he could borrow.

Well, the farmhouse was further away than he'd thought. The sun was setting, and clouds were gathering ominously in the sky. It began to get dark. The driver began rehearsing the conversation in his mind.

"I will ask to borrow a jack, and then I'll have to run back and change the tyre before it gets too dark."

As the man pondered this, it began to rain.

"Of course, it's raining. The farmer will take one look at the rain and decide that he doesn't want to go to the trouble of coming out to help me find the jack. I'd have to find it myself. In his shed, which is probably full of old machinery and rubbish!"

The sun set, and the sky got darker.

"So there I am, in a dark shed looking for a jack, tripping over junk every step I take. I'm cold and wet, and the farmer – who knows exactly where the jack is – is sitting in his house by the fire, drinking a hot cup of coffee!"

The man got angrier and angrier as he reflected on this injustice, and as the moon began to rise, he had another realisation.

"It's night time now, and I bet the farmer has already gone to bed. And when I knock, he's not going to want to get out of bed. He's going to pretend he can't hear me! There I'll be on his doorstep, cold, wet and tired, and he's not even going to answer the door. I'll be there without a jack after all."

Furious, the driver finally reached the farmhouse. He pounded on the door until he heard a timid voice from inside: "Who is it?"

"You know full well who it is, you selfish old goat! And I wouldn't borrow your jack if it were the last one on earth!" bellowed the driver, before he stormed off.

Still don't believe me?

JAMES WEBB

When Perfection is the Enemy of Good

23 November 2017

One of the soundbites that I picked up when I was in leadership was 'A bad decision is better than no decision'. I struggled with this because I didn't like making bad decisions. I was always much happier if I had all the time in the world to weigh up all the options and eventually come up with the perfect decision, a decision designed to solve the problem whilst inconveniencing or upsetting as few people as possible. In general, my natural state is to be paralysed by indecision.

Over time I began to understand that the advice was sound. The wrong decision was better than no decision. Withering on the vine was worse than moving forward and making a mistake. Doing nothing was, in my case, about fear, and that's no good. It was kind of a paradigm shift for me, and I'm still wrestling with it and reflecting on the consequences.

During this struggle, I began to notice how easy it was to find people who would not get involved in something unless it was perfect. An idea might be proposed, which was good but flawed, and then someone would reject the project on the basis of its flaws but follow this up by then doing nothing except acting like they had the moral high ground. Strange. Christians, with our various passions, theological preferences and hobby horses, seem particularly prone to this.

What I've come to realise is that there is no good deed, no charity, no well-meaning policy that is free from imperfection, but that cannot be used as a justification to do nothing. It's OK to have a problem with whatever project or work that we have a problem with. It's OK that we don't want to support it. It's OK, but we must make sure that we're doing something good in some other way, and meeting needs through some other venture, because otherwise when it comes down to a choice between those who do good imperfectly, and those who sit on their hands, we all know very well which side God is on.

Gath and Adullam

30 November 2017

David was not a king,

just a running man;

pursued by another

with blood on his mind.

David was not a king,

but would this running man

threaten Gath's Saul?

Would this refugee bring war?

David was not a king,

just a drooling man;

scratching with ragged nails

while royal Achish laughed.

David was not a king,

just a cowering man,

a cave, a hole in the ground,

like a beetle hid from the sun.

David was not a king,

but men sought him out;

four hundred losers,

debt, upset and probably never satisfied.

David was not a king,

beard still damp from indignity,

followed by an uninspiring mob,

and here is a man after my own heart.

Reasons to be Cheerful

07 December 2017

I cried out to God for help;

I cried out to God to hear me.

Is it possible for God to ever be far from us? Does He ever withdraw Himself? We can debate these questions all day long, but one thing is certain – sometimes it *feels* like He's withdrawn.

I thought about the former days, the years of long ago;

I remembered my songs in the night.

My heart mused and my spirit enquired:

"Will the Lord reject for ever?

Will he never show his favour again?"

On those days, we wonder if we will ever know His presence again. It seems like such a terminal condition. When you're in the desert, there's nothing but sand as far as the eye can see.

Then I thought, "To this I will appeal:

the years of the right hand of the Most High."

I will remember the deeds of the LORD;

yes, I will remember your miracles of long ago.

I will meditate on all your works

and consider all your mighty deeds.

But when I feel that distance, I remember that there have been many times in my life when God has felt impossibly close. I remember specific, life-shaping encounters; dragons being slain; explicit guidance; tears of gratitude. I remember times when God was so real to me that I cried out, "LORD, I can't imagine ever being depressed again!"

Your ways, O God, are holy.

What god is so great as our God?

You are the God who performs miracles;

you display your power among the peoples.

And I realise that someone, somewhere, is meeting with God right now. Someone is bumping into Jesus for the first time. Someone is being healed; forgiven; challenged; changed forever. Someone, somewhere in this world is in the middle of a full-on, black and white encounter with the Father's grace. God may feel distant from me right now, but I am a very small part of a very big universe. In my solitary, self-centred world I may suffer, but I have a big family. Somewhere, one of my brothers or sisters feels as close to God as they have ever felt.

I celebrate. I rejoice with this unnamed, unknown saint.

I am thankful, because I remember that although God feels absent today, He will draw near again. He always does.

When I was younger, the desert would often stretch out for days and months. But now I'm much better at finding the hidden streams. Sometimes God feels far away, but not for long.

JAMES WEBB

Some Beautiful Waste

14 December 2017

It's a picturesque time of year, as Christmas summons frosted grass and offers a horizon spotted with naked trees. But it's cold and wet, and that makes it less picturesque. In these conditions, the autumnal waste creates work. Every couple of weeks I have to pull manky, slimy leaves from the drain behind our kitchen or we get an overflow of yucky water outside. There's no Yuletide cheer in that job, let me tell you.

It's something of a shame, because it mars the beauty of those discarded leaves. When dry, those withered brown skeletons are one of my favourite things about autumn. There's something magical about a big pile of those jagged, crunchy seasonal offcuts. Granted, they become quite disgusting after a few days of being drenched in grey water, but what doesn't?

Maybe I'm alone in this, but I don't think so. It's amazing, isn't it, to live in a world where something that nature is throwing away is so magnificent.

Now, if even God's rubbish is beautiful, what does that make you?

Dude, Where's My Peace?

21 December 2017

It's been a hectic week. It's not just been the build up to Christmas, though that doesn't help, but Ruth has also had an operation which has put her out of action. It's been a one-man show round here for the past few days (she's doing well, by the way). I've also been very conscious of the fact that I need to come up with a blog post. Knowing that I have to produce genius every Thursday adds to the stress and pressure, which I don't always handle well. There have been a few moments this week when I've lost my cool, and my children have been the ones that have suffered. This morning I was reflecting on the irony: I've been stressed because I have to write about Christianity, when I should have just made it a priority to be a Christian.

I surrender my peace so cheaply. A little bit of pressure, and I burst. This time of year they call Jesus the Prince of Peace. I'm not sure that Jesus is the type of peace bringer that we want. We want an end to war, and we want some peace and quiet. I guess that one day Jesus will bring those things, but in the meantime he is an odd sort of Prince. The peace he brings doesn't depend on what's going on around us. Rather, he gives a peace that survives war – not freedom from fighting, but a quiet calm in the midst of the fighting, no matter how hectic.

I forget this, and let myself be controlled by the conflict around me. But Jesus is not just the Prince of Peace, he's also the Eraser of Guilt and the Master of Second Chances.

Merry Christmas!

No Blog Post This Week

28 December 2017

There's no blog post this week.

Sometimes life is like that – a combination of business and distractions that make it hard to find inspiration. Sometimes, when it is most appropriate to reflect is also the hardest time to reflect. Christmas, the celebration of Christ, is so full of things other than Christ that we find we've hardly noticed the manger in the corner. And as we approach a new year – a perfect time to ask ourselves some searching and difficult questions – we find that our days of full of other types of questions: "What's on TV today?" or "Are the shops open yet?"

That's where I've find myself. But I've also given myself permission to not write a blog this week, because it's actually OK. The world keeps spinning, and God keeps working, and – as I suggested last week – sometime the things that you think are holy are actually a distraction from the real work of holiness. There's a time to kneel in front of the altar, and there's a time to lose yourself in laughter with your family. Both belong to God. It reminds me of something that Dietrich Bonhoeffer said in *Letters and Papers from Prison*: "The man who is thinking of the Kingdom of God while in the arms of his wife is not doing the will of God." Celebration, love, laughter and distraction can be God's will too sometimes.

So that's why there's no blog post this week.

My Wife

04 January 2018

There was a very small window when Ruth was the more prominent one in our relationship. We were newly married and she got involved with the worship group at church, while I sat in the pew saying and doing nothing worthy of notice. In those days I was known as 'Ruth's husband'. Eventually I began preaching, and even ended up working for the church for a few months, so that was the end of that. Since those days Ruth has mostly been 'James' wife'.

I am typically the more public of the two of us, which is ironic because she is infinitely more sociable than I am, and better with people generally, but that's just one of the many crosses that she has to bear. It's also ironic because most people, when they're thanking or encouraging me for my speaking or writing, don't realise that there would be no words without her. Without her, life would have chewed me up and spat me out many years ago. I only have things to say because of the road we've travelled, and without her I wouldn't have survived the journey. She has been my best friend and my most loyal champion over the years, and without her I dread to think what kind of existence I would have had.

I don't believe that there's Biblical justification for the concept of 'soul mates', but I do believe that there are certain partners who will bring out the best in us, and who will be of almost limitless help in our journey to become more like Jesus. I also believe that when looking for a spouse, the question "Will this person help me grow, and can I help them grow?" is without a doubt the most important question to ask. I was young when I married, and I didn't know what I was doing, but I *was* pursuing God, and that shaped the many conversations that He and I had about Ruth. Knowing me as He does, He knew that she would be good for me. Ruth has been my greatest proof of God's generosity and grace.

Hide & Seek with God

11 January 2018

The best time to play Hide & Seek with your children is when they're old enough to be a bit creative with hiding places, but still small enough to be able to contort themselves into all kinds of sneaky nooks and crannies. If they're too young, they're often easy prey for even a semi-competent Seeker. I have played Hide & Seek with children who hide in the exact same spot where they hid last time; children who hide in the exact same spot where *I* hid last time; children who scream in terror and give away their position as soon as they hear "Ready or not, here I come!"; children who think that curling up in a ball in the middle of an empty room is an adequate hiding place, and children who think that I will not notice limbs or heads protruding from cupboards. Usually I pretend that they are more hidden than they actually are. Life is hard enough without having an ungenerous parent.

That first significant encounter with God is often a long and difficult journey, but once you've truly met Him, He becomes like a small child. He will engage in the odd game of Hide & Seek, but usually favours the 'curling up in a ball in the middle of the room' tactic, because – like all small children – really He wants to be found. But I have also come to realise that there are plenty of Christians who pretend not to notice Him, not because they're being an accommodating parent, but because they don't want to find Him. I'm talking about Christians who don't find the God who wants to be found because it'll ruin their sulk, or Christians who have their heads so tangled up in bad theology that they can no longer tell the difference between God and an armchair.

In a recent post I questioned whether or not God is ever far from us. In this post I am suggesting that He is often closer then we think, and can barely contain His hiddenness, but sometimes we stubbornly refuse to meet His gaze, because we prefer to hold on to our self-pity or our false view of God as some distant, impersonal chess master.

I know that life is complicated, and metaphors are often inadequate, but I also know that there are plenty of times where I am my own worst enemy and that, if I'm honest, there are times when I've chosen to avoid God and I'd rather pretend that it was His fault.

What's a Father to Do?

18 January 2018

Being a dad is tricky, and I don't always get it right, so when I do it tends to stick in the mind.

One Australian summer's day, at the local pool, a young Calvin came to me with a two dollar coin that he'd found. "What should I do with this, dad?" he asked, and in a moment of inspiration I replied, "Well, what do *you* think you should do with it?" He thought for a second before declaring that he thought that he should hand it in at the office. "OK, good boy, off you go and do that," I told him. He'd done a good thing, and he'd decided to do it by himself with minimal input from me. For a father, that's a satisfactory result. I sat back, warmed by the sun and the inner glow of a job well done.

The goal of a sensible father is to develop a measure of independence in his child; a level of maturity that means that she is able to give a good answer to the questions that life throws at her without needing a stage prompt every time. A man of 25 who is unable to make a decision without ringing his parents for guidance every time is still a child.

We recognise this, and know that what we want for our own children is growth and independence, yet we think that God wants something less for us. God's desire is for mature children, for us to immerse ourselves in His character so that our hearts begin to beat along to His rhythm. Then we'll find ourselves acting out His nature without needing to think about it, or even – heaven forbid! – go away and pray about it. This is exactly the thrust of Paul's discourse in Galatians 3:23-4:7, where he is arguing that we should cut the apron strings that tie us to the Law Nanny, and instead go out into the world as responsible children, making mature decisions on our Father's behalf in the family business.

I'm sure we've all had times when we've screamed "What should I do!?" at God, and all we get is silence. Has it ever occurred to you that it may not be silence as such, but rather the patience of a good father, who is actually saying, "Well, what do *you* think you should do?"; a father who is waiting to see your response and is just bursting for an opportunity to shout out a "Yes! Well done!"

And Lead us not into Temptation, but Deliver us from Evil

25 January 2018

Last week our church had a Week of Prayer and asked a few people to write a short, daily reflection on one line of The Lord's Prayer. I'm re-posting mine here.

Those of you who woke up this morning and said, "You know what I want – a random e-mail discussing the merits of various Biblical translations," can breathe a sigh of relief. Your prayers have been answered.

Today's verse is often translated as above ("And lead us not into temptation…") which is accurate enough, but can be misleading. As written it sounds like God is the one who leads us into situations where we're tempted to sin. If you flip forward a chunk of pages in your Bible you'll come to the letter written by James, and before you've finished his first chapter you'll have been told that no-one should say "God is tempting me," because that's not how God operates.

Better, or at least more helpful, translations don't mention 'temptation' but use terms like 'hard testing' or 'time of trial', which get across that idea that we're not praying for God to stop tempting us, but rather we're asking God to keep us from those difficult and awkward times where we are more likely to fall into sin. I quite like *The Message* translation here, "Keep us safe from ourselves and the Devil," which captures nicely the idea that in times of hard trial, our enemy is not God but our own weakness.

But we have another enemy of course, whom we're to pray about. Believing in a personal, literal Devil can seem superstitious these days, but you can't read the New Testament without coming away with the clear message that there is a personal force trying to work against what God is doing in the world. There are those who are too busy to pray, and there are those who are too embarrassed to pray as though the Devil is real. Jesus was neither of those.

I think that in one line of prayer, Jesus is cleverly reminding us not just to bring our struggles before God, but also that we are fighting a spiritual battle against two foes – our own fallen nature, and the evil around us that is constantly trying to undo the victory that God has already won. But perhaps the reason why this is the last thing that Jesus tells us to bring before God is because it should never be our primary focus. A healthy spirituality acknowledges the reality of both the internal and the external struggle, but is obsessed with neither.

Anyone for Seconds?

01 February 2018

Daisy wiped the tear from her cheek with a perfect white handkerchief.

"I know you all understand my struggle. It's just so…so hard," she said. "Oh, that sounds silly. To say it's 'hard'. I just don't know any other word."

"It's a perfectly good word," said Thomas, reaching out and patting her on the shoulder.

"And it's perfectly accurate," said Maureen, her lips stretched in a thin line. Daisy nodded glumly.

Maureen continued. "That's why we're here. To support and help one another. We all understand. We're all in the same boat here at the *Over Eighteens*."

The *Over Eighteens* had been meeting weekly at Thomas's house for the past year. There were seven of them. Daisy, Maureen and, of course, Thomas were the founding members. Billy (no-one called him William) and his wife Trish joined soon after, shortly followed by George. Jayne (yes, that was how she spelled it) was new to the group. This was her first meeting.

Every Thursday morning they gathered around the coffee table in Thomas's lounge, squeezed onto sofas (and chairs brought in from the dining room) and encouraged one another. That was the purpose of the group, to share and encourage, and to share and encourage in one particular struggle. The name *Over Eighteens* referred not to age, but to weight. The only thing in the group that could be called thin was Maureen's lips. Everyone bore the same burden: struggling with their size.

Thomas glanced at his watch.

"I think that's enough for today." He looked over at Jayne. "It's been excellent to have you here this morning, Jayne. We always finish with a…well, I guess you could call it a creed of sorts. We say it together, you know, to make us all feel like we're united."

Jayne nodded nervously.

"Just listen, and you'll pick it up soon enough," Thomas said, nodding at the rest of the group.

"We agree that we're overweight," the group said, in unison. "But we don't want to be. We'd like to be thin. In the meantime, we will support each other, listen to each other's struggles without judgement, encourage each other and look forward to the day when we are all our perfect weight."

Silence settled on the thoughtful group.

"Now," said Thomas, clapping his hands together, "who wants a cup of tea?"

There was a chorus of responses as Thomas stood up and moved through to the kitchen.

"You should come over for dinner sometime, love," said Trish, smiling at Jayne.

"That would be nice, " said Jayne, smiling back.

"Cor, yes, I love it when we have guests," said Billy. "Trish always goes to town with the deserts!"

"I'm surprised you have any room left for desert," interjected George. "After all, I saw how much you put away at the All You Can Eat pizza buffet yesterday!"

"You can talk!" said Billy, laughing.

Thomas returned from kitchen.

"Kettle's on," he said, placing a huge, heavy plate on the coffee table. On the plate was the biggest chocolate cake that Jayne had ever seen. "Who wants a slice?"

Hands shot up around the room. Jayne kept her hand down.

"Ummmmm," she said, as though she wanted to say something but wasn't sure how to begin.

"Go on," said Maureen, smiling with those thin lips. "Have some. Thomas is a fantastic baker."

"I'm sure he is, but…" Jayne stopped.

"But what?" said Daisy.

"Well, shouldn't we…well, I'm trying to diet." Jayne bowed her head, as though she'd confessed to some awful crime.

"Oh, of course you are," said George. "We're all trying to diet, aren't we?"

Earnest nods and grunts of agreement.

"The thing is," said Daisy. Jayne looked up to see her wiping a thick smear of chocolate icing from her cheek with that no-longer perfect white handkerchief. "The thing is, that it's difficult, isn't it?"

More nods and grunts.

"After all, that's why we're here. Because it's hard, as Daisy said earlier," said Thomas.

"We're all in favour of diets. That's what we're all after – the ultimate goal is losing weight – but it's not quite that simple, is it?" said Daisy.

"I don't know what I'd do without this group," said Trish, through a mouthful of smushed chocolate cake, "to lift my spirits and help me feel better about things."

"That's right," said Thomas, nodding. "That's absolutely right."

Jayne looked around at the group, as they grinned at her, encouragingly. She felt that she would be more encouraged if they didn't all have chocolate-stained teeth. She made a decision.

"It's been lovely to meet you all," Jayne said, standing up. "But I have to go now. The truth is, I think I'm in the wrong group."

The gathering sat in silence as she left the room. After a short moment they heard the front door slam.

"That's a shame," said Thomas. "Now, anyone for seconds?"

Based on a True Story

08 February 2018

"Good morning sports fans, I'm Rex Steele…"

"…and I'm Chuck Chuckerson!"

"…and welcome to today's event in the Parent Olympics! Who's competing today, Chuck?"

"Well, Rex, today we have James from Canterbury! He's a writer and stay-at-home dad with five children, though he's only got a couple of years experience in today's event. Remind the viewers at home what today's event is, Rex!"

"Today's event is the Post-School-Run Restoration, Chuck! The event begins when the parent returns from dropping his children off at school, and tidies up all the mess that has been made in the previous hour!"

"Sounds exciting, Rex! Now, am I right in thinking that James has already got the post-breakfast kitchen under control, so he's going to concentrate on the upstairs?"

"That's correct, Chuck! James has only been doing this event for the past couple of years, so he's still something of a rookie, but I was talking to him yesterday and reminded him that he has potentially another thirteen years of this event ahead of him, and that he should be an expert by the end of his career!"

"I expect he found that encouraging, Rex!"

"He sure did, Chuck! You can see that the bruising around my eye looks a lot better today!"

"Ha ha! Good times! WHOA, I'm going to cut you off there, Rex! James has just arrived home from the school run, and we're off!"

"He's straight upstairs, and it looks like he's heading for the bathroom! A good place to start, Chuck?"

"Good enough, Rex…And he's stepped on a soaking wet flannel that's been left in the middle of the floor! AMAZING! Can we get a slow-mo replay, on that Rex?"

"No we can't, Chuck! And WHAT A PRO! He's picked up the flannel and placed it by the sink! Now, what is that in the sink, Chuck? Some kind of exploded insect?"

"No, Rex, that's TOOTHPASTE!"

"And on the mirror and walls?"

"That's toothpaste too!"

"WOW! Those children sure cover all their bases! And what's James doing now, Chuck? Talk us through it!"

"Well, Rex, it looks like he's using the children's flannel to WIPE UP the toothpaste!"

"The flannel he just found on the floor? The one that they use to wipe their FACES?"

"That's right, Rex!"

"Ha ha, FANTASTIC, Chuck! He's really using his initiative there!"

"Now he's on to the bedrooms…wait, hang on. He's just noticed something, Rex!"

"Look at that, Chuck! The toilet roll holder is empty, I repeat, the toilet roll holder is EMPTY! Man down! MAN DOWN!"

"Thankfully, there's a fresh roll right there on top of the toilet. It won't take James long to change it, but one wonders why the child who used the last of the roll didn't change it afterwards!"

"Not really, Chuck. It's a well-known fact that children believe that changing the toilet roll causes their eyeballs to EXPLODE!"

"Job done, Rex, and James is on to the bedrooms…WHOA! Did you see that! He just ignored the bedroom belong to the teenage boys and moved straight to the bedroom of the younger kids!"

"That's right, Chuck. That's his experience kicking in – he knows that there are some battles not worth fighting."

"And he's in the bedroom now and…LOOK AT THAT! What is all that stuff? I see Lego, Playmobil and Thomas the Tank Engine toys everywhere, Rex! EVERYWHERE!"

"That's right – and don't forget the Shopkins and Barbies, Chuck!"

"Wasn't this room completely tidy when they went to bed the night before? Those are some seriously dedicated children, to have managed to get out so many toys in such a short space of time!"

"And he's moving toys round, he's tidying up, he's…he's dancing around the room? What's he doing, Chuck? He's got no time for this!"

"He just stood on some Lego, Rex!"

"Ah, OUCH…and now he's on to the beds. Is that…yes…I can see that one of the beds has not been made! One of the beds has NOT BEEN MADE!"

"And that's despite the child involved being told a MILLION times to make his bed, right, Rex?"

"That's right, Chuck, but science has proved that the louder and more often you tell a child something, the less they hear!"

"How does that work, Rex?"

"I don't know, Chuck, but it does! It's science!"

"Now James is moving away from the beds…he's not made the bed, Rex, he's NOT made the bed!"

"Uhhh, no, I think you'll find that he has, Chuck!"

"Ah. Bed making is clearly not his strong suit, then!"

"It looks like it, Chuck! Now he's almost home and free but…what's that! My WORD! Have you ever seen anything like that, Chuck?"

"James has seen it, Rex, he's seen it! It's some pyjama bottoms HANGING from a bookcase! Look at his face, Rex! Look at it!"

"Ah, yes, it's his signature expression, the 'What the Dickens…?'!"

"He's wasting time, Rex! He's got to keep moving!"

"Yes, he's got the pyjamas, Chuck, and what's that? They're COVERED in food from LAST NIGHT'S MEAL!"

"Straight to the washing basket with them, Rex! This is the last stretch! James is almost in the clear!"

"This is a good run, Chuck! He's not had to deal with some of the more time-consuming challenges like Furniture That Has Been Mysteriously Moved!"

"Or Who's Been Fiddling With The Thermostat, Rex!"

"Yes, he's at the washing basket, and he's putting the pyjamas in! This is going to be a good time…BUT WAIT! What's that? Why's he hesitating, Chuck?"

"Has he? Yes, he has! He's seen some WHITE washing in the DARK washing basket! What a nail-biting finish!"

"Yes, he's pulling out the offending item, Chuck! And I can confirm that it's some dirty underwear! I repeat, there is DIRTY WHITE UNDERWEAR in the dark washing! MY GOODNESS, Chuck! What a last minute twist!"

"And…he's put the dirty underwear in the right basket, Rex! STOP THE CLOCK!"

"And that's it! James has finished! What's the time, Chuck?"

"Oh, it's good, but it's not his best, Rex! And look, you can see the disappointment on his face! It might have been a different story without the errant pyjamas and the careless underpants!"

"Never mind, Chuck, he'll have another chance tomorrow, when he has to do it all over again!"

"That's right, Rex! And don't forget to tune in later for more exciting events from the Parent Olympics!"

"This is Rex Steele, signing off!"

"And this is Chuck Chuckerson, saying, have a fine day, sports fans!"

The Stone and the Seed

15 February 2018

I had an idea, which became this little poem. If I was an illustrator of any talent I would probably turn it into a children's picture book.

The paving stone,

set hard and set proud,

said, "I can't be moved

from my home in the ground."

"Beneath me the earth,

I crush all the life,

no root can take hold

with no hope and no light."

But a small, humble seed

a challenge did make:

"Heavy you may be,

but you've made a mistake."

The stone laughed out loud

at the tiny thing's cheek,

"You can't lift me up!

You're too small and too weak!"

"It may take some time,"

the seed did reply,

"but I'm not stuck here,

for my goal is the sky!"

The years went on by

while the seed sought a gap,

the stone did not know

of the tiny thing's trap.

And go visit now,

this is what you will see,

a humbled, broke stone

that's been split by a tree.

Imogen thought for a second, but only for a second.

"Being the best dad in the world," she said.

Smooth. She managed to palm me off while protecting Ruth's infallibility. Not bad for a five-year old. I felt quite proud of her, outsmarting her old man.

It makes me think of Abraham and Moses, the flawed saints, taking God to task for His behaviour. The passages where they argue with God would be controversial and tricky enough if it weren't for the fact that they also appear to win. We can get ourselves into all sorts of theological tangles over those passages, at least until we realise that He – being God and all – doesn't need to justify Himself to us, and we should just let Him get on with being God. He's good at it.

The point is, I believe that He must have felt a sense of fatherly pride as his children went toe-to-toe with Him because they believed in people.

Over the years it's been normal for my three boys to team up to try and take me down, but I've always been stronger and more cunning. However, as I watch them fill out and creep up, I know my days are numbered. Indeed, I suspect that when I'm in my dotage, I'm going to spend a lot of time being tipped out of my wheelchair.

I also think of Jacob, wrestling God to a standstill and extracting a blessing for his troubles. As Jacob limped away from the scene of the battle I like to think of God in heaven, nudging the angels.

"Did you see my boy go? Did you see him? What a fighter!"

Sometimes God tests us purely to give us a chance to make Him proud. I think that's a healthy way to view things – those test are not occasions to let God down, but rather occasions to bring a smile to His face.

JAMES WEBB

As One with Authority

01 March 2017

"When Jesus had finished saying these things, the crowd were amazed at his teaching, because he taught as one who had authority, and not as their teachers of the law."

Matthew 7:29

In Jesus' time, appealing to someone else's authority was a key tool of the religious teacher. A rabbi would thread quote after quote from well-regarded predecessors to give his words weight. For whatever reason this didn't resonate with the crowd, but Jesus – one who never appealed to religious tradition – had them spellbound. He, they said, had an authority that other teachers didn't.

Modern preachers and teachers rely on the authority of the Bible, but there must also be a personal authority to the words that we bring, otherwise there's no point. I'm sure we've all sat through sermons where the Bible said all that needed to be said, and the preacher should have just sat down after the reading. The messenger must bring something to the encounter, or go home.

Some preachers misunderstand what the authority of the Bible is, and treat it like an academic journal to be quoted from. They fill their sermons with verse after verse, like footnotes in an essay, and their own words serve no purpose other than to connect a string of unrelated texts. You'll know you've heard a sermon like that, because despite being full of Biblical references, it sounds like theoretical musings rather than something heavy with life and power. Remember that the piling up of quotes to support a position was how the teachers of the law did their business. People can tell that there is no real authority in such words.

Instead, every single sound from your mouth should be pulsing with the vitality of the Bible, by virtue of being a message that's consistent with the beating heart of God's word. When you do this, then your teaching will be thoroughly Biblical without even needing to quote chapter and verse.

When I was on the other side of the world and would sit and listen to people like Laurie, Pete, Paul and the rest talk about sharing Jesus' message, their words had authority. This was because they were talking about things that they knew – not things that they just knew *about* (though they did), but things that they *knew*. They shared from the overflow of their own experience, and that gave their words an authority that cannot come from heavily leaning on someone else's knowledge.

When Jesus taught about the Kingdom of God, he was talking about something that he knew, something that he had experienced. When he spoke about God and the divine vision for creation, Jesus was sharing from his own life. His words had authority not because he knew a lot about God, but because he *knew* the Father. No mental gymnastics were required. Likewise, if we want to teach as one who has authority, we too must *know* what we're teaching about.

Love is not Fair

8 March 2018

Soon I'm going to have to book a family trip to the dentist. Last time Parker refused to have his teeth checked. We'd let him know about the visit well in advance, and he seemed fine on the day itself, so we were caught off-guard by his spirited rejection of the dentist – the irony being that he is probably the child who needs a dental check-up the most. To the dentist's credit, he was reluctant to push the issue lest Parker end up traumatised. As for me, well, I was ready to kneel on his chest and prise his mouth open with my bare hands by the end of the visit. Don't worry – I didn't get that far.

It didn't end there. After we left the dentist Parker had another full-blown tantrum, this time accusing Ruth and I of not letting him go to the dentist, and blaming us for the fact that all his teeth were going to rot and fall out. You've got to laugh, haven't you? Haven't you? HAVEN'T YOU???!!!

This time I've offered him Lego if he has his teeth checked, and that might do the trick. To his brothers and sisters it looks like he's being rewarded for performing simple tasks, but there you go. I'm sure that they know that life is not fair. I've been very careful to make that clear to them on several occasions.

It is hard for them. I do wonder if, through their eyes, autism looks like fun. You get praised for run-of-the-mill behaviour, and don't get punished nearly as much as it seems you should. But if they understood autism they wouldn't wish to be in Parker's shoes. Free Lego doesn't seem like much of a trade-off when you think about all the extra complications he's going to have to negotiate in order to form meaningful adult relationships or perform to the best of his ability in everyday situations.

I hope that my children realise something important – that loving everybody the same means loving everybody differently.

Love, by its nature (and I'm talking about proper, getting-your-hands-dirty, self-denying love here) means doing what is right for each individual according to his or her needs, strengths and weaknesses. Love is personalised. Life isn't the only thing that's not fair, because if love was fair it wouldn't be love. One size most definitely does not fit all.

Some people, by the time that they get to my age, have been beaten around the head by life so badly that it's left some pretty deep scars. I know that what God expects of them is different to what He expects of me. I know that sometimes He's a bit harder on me than He would be on others, but equally I know that there are things He lets *me* get away with. However, I wouldn't for one second suggest anything other than that God loves us all with the same burning, self-sacrificial, personalised passion.

Fairness is all right for robots and pets, but children deserve something better.

Another Lost Argument

15 March 2018

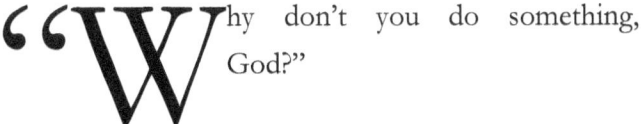

"**W**hy don't you do something, God?"

"Like what?"

"Well, I don't know. Something. Anything!"

"What's the matter?"

"There's someone who really needs to know that you love them, God. Someone who really needs your help."

"What should I do, then?"

"Well, something that makes them feel loved."

"Like what?"

"Well-"

"Should I give them a hug, perhaps? Write them a note telling them that I'm thinking of them? Give them a gift?"

"I suppose-"

"Sometimes all it takes is a smile, you know. Someone smiling at you can make a lot of difference. Should I smile at them, James?"

"I-"

"Because I do. You know that, right? You know that. How about a kind word? That can work wonders. A timely dose of kindness to a wounded soul can turn a broken man into a saint, can't it? Or have you forgotten that whole pear thing?"

"No, but-"

"Every day I whisper love to people's hearts. Sometimes I shout. But people aren't always listening. There are always so *many* other things they'd rather listen to. And I made a decision a long time ago, a decision to delegate. Delegation is an act of trust, which is an act of love, you see."

"I know-"

"And I could, I could reach out my arms and take the whole world into a hug, and draw it near to my beating heart and drown out everything else with my love, I could, and one day I will, but for now I have no arms and I have no smile. I gave those things away, James. I gave those things away a long time ago. Do you know who I gave them to, James? Do you?"

"I think-"

"That's right. I gave them to you, and your brothers and sisters. I didn't just give you peace and forgiveness and hope, I gave you responsibility. I gave you my arms and my feet and my smile and I said, 'Here you go. You're in charge of these now. Use them wisely.' I *delegated*."

"All right, I-"

"I *am* at work, James. I'm always speaking, always reminding a stubborn world that I'm here. But I've got an idea, James, about this person who needs to know my love. Do you want to hear my idea?"

"..."

"Do you, James?"

"Yes, God."

"Well then, here it is. Are you ready?"

"Yes, God."

"Why don't *you* do something?"

The Music of Easter

22 March 2018

We had nice weather last Friday. It was somewhat glorious, to be able to collect the children from school without needing to wear a coat. Spring is at hand, despite the best efforts of the weather system known as The Beast from the East, who has been trying to prolong winter. Winter, I think, is always trying to hold back spring. It won't work though. You can't stop the changing seasons.

Easter is also at hand. If you listen, you can already hear the Palm Sunday crowd, its praises echoing forward through time. The Pharisees tried to stop it, their own little Beast from the East tantrum, but that didn't work either. It's no wonder that we can hear it all, two thousand years later. Jesus himself said that if the crowd didn't get it out of their system then the stones themselves would have to take up the song; it's just that powerful.

Later that week, there was more music, though it was more muted. After their last meal together, Jesus and his friends sang a song before heading towards the garden. A glimpse of spring on the darkest night of the year. Winter tries its luck again: "The one I kiss, he's the one that you want."

And it seems to work. The friends scatter. Jesus is tried by a kangaroo court and nailed up to die.

But you can't hold back the changing seasons, and you can't hold back the magic of Easter song. Even in the darkness of Gethsemane night; the darkness of that Friday eclipse; the darkness of the tomb, we know what's coming.

The ice is thawing, the green shoots are peeking through. For us, spring will turn into summer and summer into autumn and autumn back into winter, but as far as Easter is concerned, winter is behind us and always will be.

Upside Down Food

29 March 2018

Today we remember the Passover that Jesus shared with his friends before his death; that moment when Jesus took physical, created things and imbued them with a clearly defined spiritual significance. Whatever you call it, Communion, the Eucharist, the Lord's Supper, it has its roots in the bread and wine of this final meal.

Across the world and across history, the Church has regularly remembered this moment, born in the anguish of the Last Supper. It's ironic that while we devote so much of our efforts to fleeing from suffering, we repeatedly return to this bittersweet moment because we know that it is here that God places something special into His creation.

When I did my Master's degree, I wrote my dissertation on suffering, because I thought that if I was going to have to write a dissertation, it should be on a topic that was going to be useful for pastoral ministry. Suffering seemed like a pretty obvious subject to look at. One of the things that I've learnt is that, like Communion, suffering only makes sense through the eyes of faith. Without faith, the bread and wine is just food and drink. Without faith, the cross is just a scene of injustice. Without faith, suffering is pointless. With faith, however, the bread and wine become heralds of a perfect future. With faith, the cross becomes the ultimate victory. With faith, suffering becomes a place where God meets us and does His work.

This is Easter! It's the moment when God took the worst that the Enemy could throw at Him and turned it on its head. It's the moment when suffering becomes the vehicle of salvation. And Easter is every moment in your life when you look at suffering through the eyes of faith.

"Peace Be With You"

05 April 2018

(Once again our church sent out some daily reflections over the Easter period. Below is the short piece that I wrote for Easter Sunday.)

While they were still talking about this, Jesus himself stood among them and said to them, "Peace be with you."

Luke 24:36

Sometimes I just don't get Jesus. I mean, there the disciples are, having a conversation (and they were hidden away, so it was a private conversation), when all of a sudden Jesus appears and says, "Peace be with you." I mean, I was always taught that it was rude to interrupt, but Jesus doesn't seem to care. He intrudes and cuts them off in the middle of their discussion to offer them something that they hadn't even asked for, like one of those annoying cold calls in the middle of dinner.

If Jesus really wanted to help, surely he would have gone out and about in Jerusalem and made sure that everyone saw him. Maybe he could have walked up to Herod's palace, or Pilate's residence, and knocked on the door with his nail-pieced hand and given them a telling-off. Then everyone would know that the disciples were right, and they wouldn't have to hide any more, and everyone would want to listen to what they had to say.

Instead, he arrives when they are least expecting it, and gives them – of all things – peace. Peace is all right, I suppose, but what good is peace when everyone thinks you're a heretic and wants you arrested? What good is peace when your whole world has been turned upside down, and you're about to undertake the most incredible and demanding adventure you've ever known? And when Peter and the other disciples stood there, in the future years, awaiting their own violent deaths because they had followed Jesus, do you think that they stood there and said, "Thank goodness that at least I have peace."?

I mean, is that the best thing that you can think of? The thing that you would want? For Jesus to intrude unexpectedly in the middle of your doubts and questions and struggles and say, "My peace I give to you. I do not give as the world gives. Do not let your hearts be troubled."? Is that really what the resurrection story is about? Is that really what we're supposed to do with Easter during the rest of the year?

Yes. Yes, it is. "In this world you will have trouble," said Jesus, "but take heart, for I have overcome the world." Because of Easter, Jesus is able to interrupt any struggle, any difficulty, any challenge and bring peace. You might prefer him to take away your problems, but he never promised that. Instead, he brings something better. Peace in the midst of problems. We need Jesus to intrude and offer us this peace, because there's nowhere else that it can be found.

JAMES WEBB

Throw Away Encouragements

12 April 2018

I am in favour of throwaway encouragements. A throwaway encouragement is a kind word that you slip into conversation, and then move on. A throwaway encouragement is not given in response to someone fishing for compliments. Part of its magic comes from it being unexpected. Furthermore, it must not be dwelt upon – it is given in passing and then the conversation moves on. The hearer is not given a chance to respond. Finally, it must also be true. Insisting that a tone-deaf person is actually a fantastic singer is an unkindness, both to the recipient of the lie and the victims of their newly encouraged talent.

Throwaway encouragements are one way of fulfilling Paul's injunction to be kind to one another. They can be an unexpected lift to someone's day; but more than that, they can actually be the catalyst for a significant change in someone's thinking. Often, we are blind to the things that are obvious to everyone around us, or get stuck in a pattern of seeing things a certain way, and a throwaway encouragement may be the crowbar that springs open a new door.

If you know someone quite well, I'm sure that you can think of a smash and grab positive to dump into their lap while you're on your way somewhere else. I believe that you have the potential to make a real difference to the people who cross your path. Now, let's talk about something else, shall we?

Five Random Thoughts on the Subject of Trusting God

19 April 2018

Here are five random thoughts on trusting God:

1) Trusting God to be faithful is like trusting the sun to be hot. It seems like a sure thing in theory, and we're very happy to say that we believe it to be true, but we're also really hoping that we can get through life without having to prove it.

2) I suffer from Truster's Remorse. It's that feeling you get when you actively take steps to trust God, but then you worry that the warm glow on the horizon is not the welcoming hearth-fire of heaven, but rather just your bridges burning.

3) Sometimes I wish that I could pin God down before trust is required. It would be nice, for example, to have His signature at the bottom of an iron-clad contract before taking steps. However, I know for a

fact that He prefers clay to paper. Plus I hear rumours that it's possible for even lawyers to be saved.

4) When I reflect on those times that I've trusted God with something big – I mean really trusted and not just paid lip-service to the concept of trust – I'm forced to admit that He's never let me down. Well, except for that one time in 2015 when I really wanted Him to do something specific and He did something else instead. He never seems to like my ideas.

5) C.S. Lewis was on to something when he wrote, "We are not necessarily doubting that God will do the best for us; we are wondering how painful the best will turn out to be." I'm not really afraid of trusting God, rather I'm afraid that trusting God will mean having to follow Him down some dark paths. So it becomes a question not of trusting God to keep His promises, but rather trusting Him to not break me along the way. If God can be trusted in this way, then I have nothing to worry about. But if I can't trust Him with my life , then it's time to find a new God, don't you think?

Psalm 139 for the Modern Pulpit

26 April 2018

O LORD, you have searched me
and you know me.

2 You know when I sit and when I rise;

you perceive my thoughts from afar.

3 You discern my going out and my lying down;

you are familiar with all my ways.

4 Before a word is on my tongue

you know it completely, O LORD.

5 But I think that what you're doing is illegal,

O LORD.

6 I'm pretty sure you need my permission

to hold my personal information.

7 It's a violation of my human rights

or something.

8 At the very least it's a violation of my personal space.

9 It's called stalking, and it's actually against the law, you know;

10 I don't want you following my every move, O LORD.

11 I would take out a restraining order if I could.

12 But I don't know how that works on someone who's omnipresent.

13 There was that guy who sued Google for his right to be forgotten;

so that people couldn't know his past.

14 And there's been all the stuff on the news about Facebook recently.

15 Even Mark Zuckerberg is being held accountable now.

16 Who said that you were allowed to remember everything about me, O LORD?

Who holds you accountable?

17 I don't care if you created my inmost being;

or knit me together in my mother's womb.

18 That doesn't give you the right to invade my privacy.

19 And you say that all the days ordained for me were written in Your book…

20 Actually, that sounds like a threat;

Are you threatening me, O LORD?

21 My business is my business;

My life is mine and mine alone.

22 And it's none of your business what I do with it.

23 Or what I do in the privacy of my own home.

I don't want you knowing everything I do.

24 I'd rather be anonymous than have you close, O LORD.

A King of Two Halves

03 May 2018

I've been doing some work for a sermon on Jesus as the Messiah, and it got me thinking. Israel had been waiting and watching for the Messiah for hundreds of years and when he finally appeared they missed him, because he wasn't the sort of Messiah they were looking for. They had been expecting a great political and military leader to set the nation's wrongs right – a new King David. What they got was a homeless preacher who was obsessed with healing the sick and lacked nationalistic zeal. What I realised yesterday was that the Old Testament makes it kind of obvious exactly how the Messiah would follow in David's footsteps.

David's kingship is a story of two halves. His rise to the throne is told in 1 Samuel, and is full of some very well-known stories. David slays Goliath and flees from Saul, fearing for his life, and eventually forgiving the man who persecutes him. He faces many obstacles, but the theme that comes through is best spelt out in 1 Samuel 30:6 – 'David was greatly distressed because the men were talking of stoning him…But David found strength in the LORD his God.'

By contrast, the story of David's kingship in 2 Samuel and 1 Chronicles is very different. Although he achieves many important things, the stories that stand out from David's reign are not like those that went before. Instead, we hear about his adultery with Bathsheba and murder of her husband; his trust shifting from God to his army; being told that he will not build the temple because he has too much blood on his hands; a brutal civil war because he was a bad father to Absalom. These are all things that happened after David reached the pinnacle of power. Yes, he was a great leader and a godly man, but the Old Testament isn't shy about his failings. It's almost as if those who compiled the stories want to say that David, the refugee shepherd of misfits, trumps David, the mighty warrior king, every time.

If the people of Israel had seen that, then they might have been able to make sense of Jesus. Of the two halves of the great king's story, it makes perfect sense that the Messianic Son of David would base his life on the first. After all, Jesus himself said that it was the poor in spirit who would lay hold of the Kingdom of God, not the influential power brokers. I have to confess that I can't understand those Christians who think that the best way to further God's purposes is from the throne, from a position of strength and power. I wonder if they've even ever read their Bibles.

Five More Thoughts on the Subject of Trusting God

10 May 2018

I think that there are at least five different types of God to trust. Which one do you put your hope in?

1) <u>The Enabler of Spoilt Children.</u>

This God owes you. Everyone knows that when this God says things like, "But seek first the kingdom and my righteousness, and all these things will be given to you as well," what He's really saying is, "What do want for Christmas?" When life doesn't go well, it is this God's fault – after all, didn't He say He'd look after you? Following this God is like being on a roller coaster, dipping and climbing between feelings of confident entitlement and angry disappointment.

2) <u>The One Who Doesn't Really Mean It.</u>

This God, like everyone else in your life, will let you down. He makes promises all the time, but doesn't deliver. The only thing you can be certain of is that He won't come through for you. He's like a lifeguard who encourages you to dive headfirst into the pool, with no intention of jumping in after you when you get out of your depth. Trusting this God turns you into a nervous swimmer, stuck on the side of the pool, unable to put even a toe into the water.

3) The Master of the Monkey's Paw.

This God keeps his promises, but in an unexpected and unpleasant way, like one of those horror story genies who gives you exactly what you asked for. He is a trickster who needs to be outsmarted rather than trusted. You've accepted that your best bet for happiness is to try and manipulate the small print in order to get a positive outcome. Believing in this God leads to a crushed, submissive spirit that is constantly expecting to be punished '…for your own good.'

4) The Divine Bureaucrat.

This God also keeps his promises, but only to the letter of the law. You will get what you're entitled to – nothing more, nothing less. He is always busy figuring out how little He can give away without being sued for breach of contract. Under this God, the Bible becomes a watertight legal contract. Trusting this God leads to low expectations, and a feeling that He needs to be backed into a corner before he'll reluctantly dish out bread and water and expect you to be grateful for it.

5) The Real Deal.

This God can't be contained by small words like 'gracious' and 'generous'. To this God, the promises that are written in the Bible reveal His heart without defining the limit of it. He believes that it is possible to be kind without needing to announce it first, and that children can have birthday presents even though nothing has been submitted in writing beforehand. Following this God will get you into trouble, but the good kind of trouble, and eventually you'll be able to face whatever life throws at you with a quiet confidence and hope.

Fellow Pilgrims

17 May 2017

Crowded together on this train, heading to the city;

Only this is taking much longer than I had hoped.

Nobody seems to care about my needs;

Sitting there, with their loud conversations, loud music, loud chewing.

I can't believe this is happening.

Do you hear him? He's singing along to the music on his headphones!

Enjoy the music, go on! Don't consider what I might want;

Really, all I want to do is read my book in peace.

Oh, now what's this? Another stop at another station.

There's a man getting on. I hope he doesn't sit next to me;

He's, shall we say, rather on the large side. I bet he smells too.

Everyone's smiling, watching as he makes his way down the carriage;

Right and left, right and left, he looks for an empty seat, and stops next to me.

Sure, sit right down why don't you? What else could go wrong?

Bad parents, messy eaters, I've got them all;

Everyone, it seems, is out to ruin my day.

This would be a really nice journey if it weren't for them.

The headphone singer seems to be getting louder;

Even Gandhi would have punched this guy by now.

Relaxing, this ain't!

This is the worst group of people I've ever had the misfortune to meet;

How did I end up in a carriage with them?

All we've got in common is our destination;

Now I'm expected to put up with all their nonsense?

You've got to be kidding me!

Our friend, Mr Fatty, has fallen asleep!

Unbelievable! His head's on my shoulder! My shoulder!

Right away he starts to snore.

Somebody help me – I think he's about to start drooling.

Every time I think I'm going to get some peace, someone like this comes along;

Let's agree that, in future, I should only travel with a certain type of people;

Very nice, clean, good-looking, low maintenance people.

Everyone, in other words, who's like me.

Stuck on this journey together, they could at least put my needs first.

Noises that Sound Good

24 May 2018

I am not musical but I love music; it's such a clever idea – noises that sound good. Also, I like it when people put words to the backdrop of said music. I believe that they're called 'songs'.

Like most people, I have my own personal taste in music, but it's a taste that seems to put me at odds with the Christian majority, a fact I find hard to believe. Surely I can't be the only one who thinks that most church services could be improved by the introduction of some Dubstep?

When I was a teenager in the 90s, the Christian music I was familiar with didn't do anything for me. As for the lyrics? Well, let's just say that I felt more of a spiritual kinship with someone like Kurt Cobain than I ever did with Matt Redman or Martin Smith. One of the best things that ever happened to me at university was meeting Terry Wright. During Fresher's Week, Terry sat next to me in a chapel service purely because I looked like the type of person who was into the same music as he was. He was wrong, but only because I had never heard anything like it before. Terry had an extensive knowledge and collection of alternative Christian noise from such labels as Frontline, R.E.X. and (my own personal choice of the mid-to-late 90s) Tooth & Nail. It was a revelation to hear these bands playing music more to my tastes, and singing about their faith in a way that resonated with my bruised and growing soul. Take, as a random example, a simple verse from *The Prayer Chain*'s song, 'Dig Dug':

Can you hear my heart beat?

Do you even know my heart?

When I hold the doubts of Thomas

As hard as I hold your promise?

I never heard anything like that sung on a Sunday morning, but it was exactly the sort of honesty that I was desperate for at the time. Although I am no longer the angsty teenage nightmare that I was then, I know that a lot of the music I listened to during that time has supported me through my difficult journey over the years, and still provides the foundation for my own personal expressions of worship. I might write a bit more in the future about specific albums and songs that have been meaningful to me, but I've wanted to write something like this for a while; partly to share something that has been influential and might give a bit of insight as to why I write the way I do, plus also as a belated thanks to Terry for first exposing me to those particular noises that sounded so good.

The God of All Comfort

31 May 2018

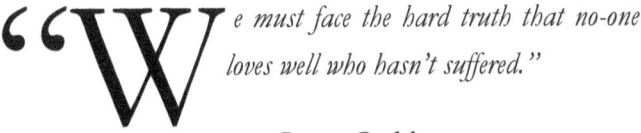

"*We must face the hard truth that no-one loves well who hasn't suffered.*"

Larry Crabb

"Praise be to the God and Father of the Lord Jesus Christ, the Father of compassion and the God of all comfort," writes Paul to the Corinthians, "who comforts us in all our troubles, so that we can comfort those in any trouble with the comfort we ourselves have received from God." It's a bit of a mouthful, and Paul certainly wouldn't get a good mark in any writing class (far too many 'comforts'), but hopefully you get his point.

In case you don't, it's this: suffering isn't all about you. One of the tricks that suffering plays on our mind is to make us even more self-focused; we struggle to see beyond our own painful situation. God, however, has His own tricks, and one of them is to turn suffering on its head by making it about how we can help others. Tell me, do you think the Enemy likes it when God disarms his great weapons so completely? Suffering equips you to love in a way that a life free from unpleasantness doesn't.

"For just as the sufferings of Christ flow over into our lives," Paul continues, "so also through Christ our comfort overflows." If your goal is a life free from suffering then don't bother with Jesus – he'll just get in your way. If, however, your goal is a meaningful life then realise that suffering is not just part of the journey, but a key part of the process, and one that you are not alone in. Don't get distracted. Offer your experiences to those around you who are troubled. In this way suffering can be turned into comfort.

Skimming the Sun

08 June 2017

I had a thought the other day.

There is really only one story – God's story.

You and I create stories, but the only bits that will last are those that reflect the heart of God's story. I don't mean that only stories that talk explicitly about God are the only ones with any value, rather a tale's worth depends on how much it reflects the story from which all other stories flow. Give me any day a yarn spun by an atheist with the scent of heaven in his nostrils rather than another two-dimensional moral diatribe written by someone with a fiery pen and a cold heart!

God's story burns at the centre of the solar system, orbited by every other story ever created. There are stories that are popular and lauded, but are really nothing more than lifeless, icy rocks spinning out into the infinite void. Then there are others, small and ignored, that rotate so close to the sun that they burn with a lover's passion and can't be seen without looking at the source itself.

I hope that, whenever I write and whatever I write, I am in some way honouring the story that keeps me warm at night.

"Since all the world is but a story, it were well for thee to buy the more enduring story, rather than the story that is less enduring." – St. Columba

One Trick Pony

14 June 2018

I think that, for many years now, I've really only had one message. I think about the lectures I've given, sermons I've preached and stories I've told in the recent past and – to me – they're mostly variations on a single theme. My life consists of repeated attempts to find different ways of saying the same thing over and over again. It makes sense to me; I'm definitely more of a 'Do one thing really well rather than lots of things badly' personality type. It's also something I can imagine God saying to me: "James, I'm giving you one message to proclaim. Just the one, but it's an important one. I don't think you're quite up to handling several things at once. Be as creative as you want in sharing that message, but try to stay on focus, OK?"

I'm sure that there are plenty of people who are expected to multitask, but it also seems totally consistent with God's love of community that He would share the work out among His children rather than overload one or two and let the rest spend the day at the beach. Billy Graham is, I think, an example of someone who had just one job, and good things happened when he made that his priority. Pay careful attention to that desire to have a finger in every pie, because maybe it was never your pie in the first place. It's just rude to stick fingers in pies that don't belong to you.

So, what's the one thing that God has given you to do or say? It certainly helps to know what it is, and you could do a lot worse than doubling down on it.

And the one message I've been repeating for the past decade or so? Well, I'm not going to just come right out and tell you what it is here, am I? Where's the fun in that?

The Best Defence is a Good… Silence?

21 June 2018

I've been reading, which gets me thinking, and thinking gets me into trouble. I've been thinking about how quick we are, when criticised or challenged, to leap to our own defence. I suspect we're motivated by wounded pride rather than a sense of injustice – after all, are we quite as quick to jump to the defence of another?

When Jesus stood before his accusers he made no attempt to justify or acquit himself. He offered only silence, sprinkled with brief answers to questions. No "Let me explain…"; no "Let me tell you my side of the story…"; no "It was their fault!"; no outrage, shock or fury. Just silence. But is that really realistic? Isn't this just an extreme example tied to the necessity of the crucifixion? Surely, if our name is dragged through the mud, we should make every effort to put people right? Shouldn't we? Surely?

Two quotes come to mind at this point. The Chinese philosopher Lao Tzu, who said, "Those who justify themselves rarely convince." I think he makes a good point. Or then there's something I heard once from either Neil T. Anderson or Larry Crabb (I can't quite recall) that goes something like this: "If you are in the wrong you have no defence, and if you are in the right you need no defence."

But does it work in so-called real life?

I know someone who once was publicly accused. He sat in a group and listened to someone make all kinds of claims against him and his character. After his accuser had finished he stood up and said, "Well, you all know me, and you can decide for yourselves if those things are true or not," before sitting down. And that was that. There was no attempt to defend himself with words, because he had years and years of integrity and actions to speak on his behalf. No doubt there were those who would find that an unsatisfactory defence – perhaps almost an admission of guilt – but I can't help but feel that there's no response to criticism more powerful than a godly life.

Something to think about perhaps, but try not to get into too much trouble.

Father's Day

28 June 2018

And have you ever regretted those words,

spoken in light but planned in darkness?

Did it seem like such a good idea,

in those days before, when the three of you

laughed and danced and joked and sang

with delight, before delight had even been

    invented?

Did you know, when you said to each other,

"Let us make some people now, some good ones,"

that you were sentencing yourself

to years and years of dirty nappies,

bare feet on carelessly discarded Lego bricks,

and ungrateful teenagers blanking you every day?

Did you know that you would spend

sleepless nights, longing for the days

of innocence, when a grazed knee was

the worst thing in the world,

but so easily fixed with a hug, and rewarded

with the dried tears that made you feel loved?

Did you know that you would bear it all?

Every broken heart?

Every bad decision?

The death of every pure thing?

Every act of cruelty and hate, some so evil

that they leave an irredeemable scar on history?

I momentarily feel a genuine yearning for the freedom of being 'disillusioned', and seeing myself as I really am, and seeing God as He really is. I reflect, not for the first time in my life, that it's not actually much fun being a deep thinker. But we're all complicated in our own way, and we all make things more complicated than they need to be. God likes simple things, I write. I notice that I've actually written 'God likes simple things, I write'. I decide to stop before I get too clever for my own good.

The hot chocolate is gone. The street preacher might still be there. It's time for me to go. I think God probably did turn up, in some way.

McChurch

12 July 2018

elcome to St. Ronald's,

May I take your order please?

We can give you a serving of Jesus,

With an extra helping of cheese.

We can do a Resurrection Burger,

And a side of Holy Ghost fries,

As long as you like it LOUD,

We don't do any other size.

We're all about convenience,

You don't even have to stay,

No-one really likes washing-up,

That's why we do takeaway.

Sure there's other restaurants,

And other places you can eat,

But we're cheap and quick and easy,

And we won't disturb your sleep.

Don't worry about nutrition,

Or if we'll make your soul fatter,

As long as you leave feeling good,

Then quality doesn't matter.

Our menu's tailored just for you,

Our staff will help you to begin,

Our manager is God Himself,

But I'm not sure He's ever been in.

And does the pride outweigh the shame,

and the hope outweigh the despair,

for the three who trust so much?

Do you say, "That's my boy!",

or "I'm so proud of her!" when we take

our first faltering steps onto the shore?

And do you see beyond the reborn darkness,

to the flicker of light in every act of love,

so small, so frail and yet so vital?

And when you reach down and we slap your

    hand away,

is your forgiveness and patience really endless?

(Because I know mine isn't.)

And are you looking forward to that time,

when we'll finally come to our senses,

and you'll at last be buried under the weight

of all those 'Best Dad Ever!' mugs

that we made or bought in secret

with the stuff you gave us in the first place?

And do you have a knowing smile,

or a tear in your eye, as Adams and Eves,

so desperate to become gods,

discover that divinity is hard, ugly work?

Do you ever look at the stars and wonder,

these days, who'd be a father?

Meta Edition

05 July 2018

I'm sitting in a cafe, with my notebook and pen, trying to come up with something for this week's blog. I've got a hot chocolate in front of me, and I'm waiting for God to show up. Maybe He's down the road, with the street preacher, whose muffled but earnest words drift in through the open window. I feel guilty. Why aren't I out there, on the street, preaching instead of sitting here with an empty page and a hot chocolate? Mentally I list the reasons, both good and bad. I offer up a quick prayer for the young man trying to get something of God's love out into the world.

I ask myself why I feel guilty. I wonder if it's got something to do with my view of God. I imagine myself in one of those fairground mirror funhouses, but instead of rows and rows of mirrors distorting my image, I'm looking at dozens of distorted images of God. Is that what it's like? I scribble that down.

Thoughts and ideas zoom through my imagination, like wasps at a summer picnic. I spend a moment wondering if Belgian chocolate is really that much better than other chocolate, or if it's just a triumph of marketing. I go back to the funhouse mirrors, and wonder if the issue is not so much false views of

God, but rather false views of myself. I picture my own distorted image instead. That's just as much a source of misplaced guilt and confusion as distorted images of God.

I look at what I've written. I feel like there's something in the funhouse mirror idea and that I'm on the cusp of putting together a blog post, but the idea just won't firm up. It's a mist that disperses when I try to grab it. I'm distracted by the couple on the table across from me. She's reading out the titles of articles in her magazine, while her husband (I assume it's her husband) listens mutely. One of the articles is wondering about the real reason behind JFK's assassination. I wonder what magazine it is, as the couple don't look like conspiracy theorists. Maybe that's what they want me to think…

I try to get back to the blog post. I write some more thoughts down. How do we view ourselves in the mirror of guilt? How does that distort who we are? It's not real. It's not how God sees us. I pause. I feel like that's something it would be good to pray for – that I'll see myself as God sees me, as I really am. I would pray right here and now, but I've just decided that I'm going to write this process up as my blog post, and I know that I'd only be praying so that I could write it down and put it in the blog because actually praying reads better than just intending to pray.

Empty Hands

19 July 2018

Sometimes I challenge myself but more often I leave it to others to challenge me. Recently, I came across an observation made by someone else: the suggestion to pray for 'our daily bread' in the Lord's Prayer is supposed to encourage us towards a daily trust in God to meet our needs. It challenged me because I know that even when I'm asking for my 'daily bread' I'm already thinking about what I'm going to eat tomorrow. I'm not in the habit of asking God to meet my daily needs, I'm in the habit of asking Him for a surplus so that I don't have to worry about empty cupboards for the next few years. I wonder what would happen if all I ever asked for was just what I needed for that day? I know one thing it would change – It'd certainly be an incentive to check in with my heavenly Father at least once every twenty-four hours…

It made me think about 'stuff', why I worry about it and why I cling so hard to it. Sometimes I think I justify acquiring stuff by telling myself that it's another resource I can use for God's purposes. I'm not sure I'm being entirely honest with myself, and I wonder if – in my case – empty hands are more useful to Him.

I had a little thought last weekend. What if we get to heaven and God asks us to show Him our hands? What if everyone's hands look the same – damaged and battered and bruised and scarred? But what if our hands *aren't* the same? What if God knows that some of us have wounded hands because we've worked hard for Him, but others of us have wounded hands because we've been holding on to our treasure too tightly?

More Daily Bread Thinking

26 July 2018

Sometimes an idea just won't let me go, and so it has been with my thoughts about dependence on God and just asking for what we need each day.

It occurred to me that the future is often a source of anxiety and frustration for me. It doesn't have to be, but it is. Jesus understood the way that our minds work, which is why he said, "Don't worry about tomorrow, because you've got enough to worry about today." The thing is, the future is all in my head. How I think about it is what creates the anxiety and the frustration, not the future itself. Developing an attitude of relaxed, daily dependence on the Father is the cure.

This is what I have figured out: If I am thinking about the future, then what I have today isn't enough, but if I am just thinking about this day, then what I have for today is an abundance. Does that make sense? If I expect God to give me everything I need for my whole life today, then He is a stingy and unhelpful deity. If I expect God to give me just what

I need for today, then He is a generous and extravagant Father. I do not have nearly enough to get me to the end of my life (assuming I make it to old age), but He has provided ample to get me through the next twenty-four hours.

This isn't a rant against wealth or putting things aside for the future, rather it's a pointed conversation I'm having with myself about where my trust lies. If I take Jesus seriously then my focus is clear – "Put the Kingdom first, and God will take care of the rest," he said. If I'm seriously putting God and His agenda first, then I can live fearlessly with empty hands. "Father, give us what we need for today," becomes enough.

In Memory of Dick Vesey

02 August 2018

As I sit here and type this I genuinely feel like the world is a poorer place. I don't think I've ever known a calmer presence and a more gentle gentleman than Dick. Some eventful things happened to the Veseys over the years, but I don't need many fingers to keep track of the number of times I'd seen Dick anything other than serene and unruffled. I don't often write about my time at Hayward's Heath, but you shouldn't read anything into that. It's been a key part of my journey so far, and I am thankful for the experiences that I had there, and very thankful for the people that I met and worked with. The leadership team at the church was a fantastic group, and that included Dick, the ubiquitous elder, first at Sussex Road and then at Harlands.

Dick and Hilary have been generous and supportive of our family over the years. It was Dick, with his giant pastoral heart, who took it upon himself to keep me informed about the people whom we loved, and who loved us, back in Hayward's Heath while we were sunning ourselves in Australia. At

Hayward's Heath, I was blessed to be in a church that sometimes tolerated but often appreciated my experiments in preaching, but in writing this I have realised that Dick was probably one of the most ardent supporters of my pulpit adventures. I don't want anyone to feel left out, but when I think about the people who were most encouraging and positive as I wrestled with my gifting, Dick is one of the first faces to come to mind.

As is often the case, heaven's gain is our loss. We will meet again, but in the meantime we carry on. This is what it means to be the church of Christ, the body of battling believers striving to bring the Kingdom to the Now, but dreaming of the Not Yet.

Lost in Translation

9 August 2018

There are lots of different translations of the Bible. At the time of writing, the online Bible resource BibleGateway has 59 different English translations available. That's a lot of Bible, and unless you read Greek and Hebrew yourself, you're stuck with someone else's interpretation.

The fact is, all translations have strengths and weaknesses. I don't think you can argue convincingly that any translation is the One True Version, especially as – and some of you may find this hard to believe – Jesus didn't actually speak English.

In my last sermon, I referred to Malachi 4:2. The *King James Version* goes with "But unto you that fear my name shall the Sun of righteousness arise with healing in his wings…", which is a fairly literal translation of the original. Some copies of the *New International Version* plump for "But for you who revere my name, the sun of righteousness will rise with healing in its rays…", which is, I suspect, much closer to what the original author was trying to convey. However, in the context of my sermon, I needed the more literal *KJV* translation. Something was lost in the dynamic equivalence of the *NIV*, even though it is arguably the 'better' translation.

When I first made the decision to follow Jesus, I read from the *Good News Bible*. No-one reads it nowadays, but I will always have a soft spot for it because of the role it played in my early spiritual growth. Plus, I still think its translation of Proverbs is first-rate. When I was at university, the *New Revised Standard Version* was recommended to us as the best mix of readability and scholarly accuracy, so I have a copy on my shelf for that reason – but I rarely ever use it. For over two decades now, the *NIV* has been the translation I use in my everyday life. *The Message* gets a lot of stick in some circles, but Eugene Peterson's version of the Psalms is excellent, and those who turn their noses up at his scholarship might want to check out his translation of Galatians 3:23-24:

"Until the time when we were mature enough to respond freely in faith to the living God, we were carefully surrounded and protected by the Mosaic law. The law was like those Greek tutors, with which you are familiar, who escort children to school and protect them from danger or distraction, making sure the children will really get to the place they set out for."

In terms of Paul's argument, that is, hands down, the best translation of those verses I have ever read, and should certainly knock all talk of 'prisoners' and 'school teachers' on the head. If you delve deeper into the concept of the 'Greek tutor' then you can truly have your mind blown by what Paul goes on to say from chapter 3:25 to chapter 4:7…

Anyway, what I really want to ask is what your favourite translation of the Bible is, and why? Is it because it's objectively the best translation, or is it because it's the version that you grew up with, or the one that had a particular translation of a particular verse that you found especially helpful in a difficult time, or is it because someone you respect told you that it was the 'best' translation? Thankfully, the Holy Spirit is big enough and gracious enough to be found in those words, regardless of how good a version I think it is.

For the Quiet Ones

16 August 2018

I was sad to hear that Hayward's Heath Baptist Church has lost another faithful servant. Les Ridd, another who served on the leadership team with me, died at the end of last week. Like Dick, he had been ill for a while, but it doesn't make it easier.

I was thinking about Les and Dick, and what they gifted to the church, and found it simplest to put my thoughts down into one of my occasional not-poem things.

There are plenty of noisy servants.

"Where there are many words," said the Teacher,

"sin is not far behind."

(Loud men and women, we know who we are)

Many words booming from the pulpit,

or clattering onto the page

like a skip full of scrap metal.

"I tell you the truth," says Jesus.

"They have received their reward in full."

But there are also the quiet servants,

whom you have never heard,

and will maybe never even see,

(certainly not in a photo on the back of a book)

doing what they do on tiptoe.

Stacking chairs, cutting and sticking with children,

giving lifts and clearing out guttering silently in

    the background.

"I tell you the truth," says Jesus.

"For them, the best is yet to come."

Bad Examples

23 August 2018

One of the problems with having written a weekly blog for nearly three years is that you begin to lose track of what you have and haven't already written. I'd love to not repeat myself, but the chances of that are pretty small. For example, have I written about motivation before? I feel like I have, but I can't rightly recall in what context, and even after three years I still don't know WordPress well enough to do something like a keyword search of all my previous blogs.

I was thinking about motivation because I was wondering (again) how much motivation matters if the outcome is something good and worthy. I've written before about what a lazy writer I am, but if there's one thing guaranteed to motivate me it's reading a bad book that has been well received. It's happened to me on countless occasions; I pick up a book with the 'New York Times Bestseller' seal of approval and find that it's a bad book. I don't just mean a book I don't like, I mean a BAD BOOK, as in it's horribly written. Nothing motivates me to sit down and write like seeing someone get paid lots of money for doing something I think I can do better. I think that all I really need in order to actually write a thousand-page novel is a steady supply of poorly-written bestsellers, though I'll probably have gone insane by the time I have written chapter 6.

What I was wondering is, does it matter anyway? If I actually sit down and get something constructive done, does it matter if my motivation is hardly noble? Perhaps it's actually God's way of subverting my laziness, cheekily harnessing my own pride and greed? Maybe it's really a self-destructive base for my writing – after all, can I really claim that my work is worthy if it's initiated by something unworthy? And having thought about all that, what if my motivation is not really 'I can do better' but actually 'Readers deserve something better'? No answers today, just thoughts, but I can't shake the feeling that God would rather I write than didn't write. That's enough for me at the moment, and I'll let Him sort out the tangled weave of my motives when He gets round to it.

Hmmmmm. This definitely all feels familiar…

It's True

30 August 2018

Dear Reader,

I'm writing to you because there's something that I want to tell you. It's something that I overheard once, and although it wasn't originally meant for you, I thought I should pass it on, because it *is* meant for you really.

You are God's favourite.

Knowing you, there are a few different ways you might react to this news, but all of them are saying the same thing: "I don't believe it."

You might find it hard to believe because you don't think you *should* be God's favourite. You're not good enough. How can you be God's favourite when you're such a terrible person? Well, I wouldn't go that far. I certainly don't think you're a terrible person, but you're probably right that you don't deserve to be God's favourite, and yet you are.

You might be wondering, what about everyone else? Well, I'm not writing to everyone else, I'm writing to you, and I am telling you that you are His favourite.

Perhaps you're rolling your eyes right now, because you think this is typical of the rubbish that I come up with. Maybe it even makes you angry, that I would dare to write such a thing. That doesn't change anything. You're still His favourite.

Maybe you're worried about what might happen if you really believe it. Would you get too big for your boots? Would you start to look down on other people? Now, don't be silly. Do you think God is happy when we settle for a lie because we're scared of the consequences of believing the truth? If His biggest concern was us abusing or misunderstanding His words then He'd never say *anything*. No, the truth is that you're His favourite, and He wants you to know it.

And surely that's got to mean something, right? That's got to change the way that you think about yourself, and the way that you think about God, because it's true. It really is true. You are God's favourite.

Yours faithfully,

James

Talking About Yourself

6 September 2018

I'm probably the only person in the world who thinks that preachers need to tell more stories about themselves. Not only do preachers not tell *enough* stories about themselves, I also think that when they do, they tell the *wrong* stories.

Let me make up an example. Let's say that I'm listening to a sermon on evangelism. Let's also say that the preacher tells a story about a time that he had a leaking pipe in his home. He kept meaning to get round to doing something about it, but he never had the time. When he finally got to it, the persistent leaking of a single drop of water had caused some big wooden boards to rot. Imagine that the preacher then suggests that sometimes evangelism is like that – a consistent, little effort that can, over time, have a huge impact.

It's a nice image and an illustration that might be quite helpful to someone, plus it's exactly the sort of metaphor that I enjoy. Nothing wrong with that – I would happily include such a story in one of my own sermons – but maybe the congregation also needs a different story from the preacher's life? Perhaps a story in which the preacher himself tells of a situation where his own consistent, little effort made a huge difference. In other words, a story of how he put his preaching into practice?

I know very well the internal debate that comes from deciding whether or not to include a story that makes me look good, but sometimes my hesitation is just another refusal to get over myself. Refusing to share something that might be helpful to your congregation because it reveals something positive about you? Well, that's just a different way of making the sermon revolve around your ego.

When I was in Cornerstone I learnt from many men and women who shared stories of how they actually went out and *did* the things they were talking about. Sometimes it was a story of how things went wrong, but more often it was a story of how this God stuff *does actually work*. As someone who finds the theoretical easier than the practical, it was informative and inspiring. Those earthy stories that backed up the theory actually changed me, for the better. That's what a congregation needs – not just to be taught the truth, but to be inspired to live it. Stories from our lives of how we put things into practice may be the little push that encourages someone to sweep away the years of fear and act.

So preacher, tell more stories about yourself. Tell the congregation about worship that drew you closer to God, or prayers that didn't. Don't just share the disastrous attempts to explain your faith, talk about the times when you got it right. Share the tools you use to survive the moments when God seems distant, and shout from the rooftops the tales of how God showed up in your hour of need.

Of course, I do have the nagging fear that the reason we preachers don't tell many of those kind of stories is because we don't have many of those kind of stories *to* tell. In that case, perhaps we should step down from the pulpit for a while, until our actions have caught up with our words and we actually have a life to preach.

Memory Lane

13 September 2018

I have been journaling on and off since I was 18, and recently I decided to read through some of my old notebooks. There are some gaps in my history, where I had a year or so off, but on the whole it's a reliable screencap of my mental state over the past twenty years.

My initial goal was to write about things I was praying for, and record the various answers (or non-answers) that I got. It quickly became a Frankenstein's monster; entries were either me complaining to God about the fact that I didn't have a girlfriend, or some totally surreal stream of consciousness. Take for example, these nuggets from 1996:

25.4.96

Did Paul ever think that his letters would make it into the canon?

27.4.96

Q.P.R. relegated.

I mean, *what is all that about?* I certainly don't remember sustaining a brain injury while at university.

I'm exaggerating a bit, of course. There is some good stuff in there too. There are things that God did for me that I had totally forgotten about. I have vague memories of certain random people, but my journals reveal that teenage me had dutifully recorded their names and tried to pray for them over the months. I was really, really weird, but I wasn't a total lost cause.

One thing that surprised me is being able to actually *see* myself grow over the years. Even 1997 James seems a lot more stable than 1996 James (admittedly, I was going out with Ruth by then, so the number of "What's wrong with me? Why haven't I got a girlfriend?" entries decrease considerably). 1997 James actually says some stuff I agree with, and I see in him the genuine passion for God that 2018 James believes has sustained him over the years. Reassuringly, the growth gets more and more pronounced as we go along, until 1996 James seems unrecognisable.

Some of the things that I have written in my journals I no longer believe, and some of them are just downright embarrassing, but I am thankful for the investment I made in the habit. It's amazing to watch maturity sneak up on a wobbly teenager who was armed with nothing more than a desire for God and an interest in where Q.P.R. finished each season. I'm thankful to be able to put flesh on the bones of half-remembered stories, and to have a record of exactly *when* God said *what*.

And 2018 James has turned out alright.

Seven Thoughts for Preachers

20 September 2018

Here are seven thoughts for preachers:

1) The Bible contains poetry, exposition, theological analysis, parables, historical accounts, song and more. Valid styles of preaching are just as varied; a.k.a. The 'More than one way to skin a cat' Principle.

2) Which style of preaching is the style most likely to get your heart racing and the blood pumping through your veins? That's probably the style of preaching that you should be attempting.

3) Preaching is *not about you*, and preaching is *all about you*. Understand this paradox in the following way: Bring the unique fingerprint of God's image in you to your listeners, while doing all you can to not inflict the unique flaws of your sinful nature on them.

4) Read Ephesians 4:7-13 carefully. It is not the preaching that is the gift, but the preacher. Would your congregation describe you as a gift?

5) Passion, communication skills, and an understanding of the psychology of storytelling? Excellent. Emotionalism, being clever for the sake of being clever, and manipulation? Not so much.

6) One of the best skills a preacher can learn is discerning when being mocked, misunderstood and ignored is your own fault, and when it is just a Romans 8:17 thing (you only get to share in Christ's glory if you share in his sufferings).

7) You need to put into words what God is already trying to teach His people, rather than what you think they need to learn. Therefore, the best preachers are the ones who know how to listen.

Alone in the Dark

27 September 2018

I'm currently working on a project where one of the main characters had to make her way through an underground cavern where there was no light. She was supposed to feel her way through the darkness, towards the exit. It marks something of a transition for the character, like all clumsy overused metaphors in stories do. But a strange thing happened while I was writing the scene. I threw in a line that just felt right and it totally changed things. You see, it turned out that she wasn't alone in the cavern. She was supposed to be alone, but the story wasn't happy with that. It turned out that, in the blackness, she wasn't by herself after all, and that made things much more interesting.

Travelling through the darkness alone was supposed to be just a challenge the character overcame in order to get to where she needed to be, but there's something about someone making your way through a dark cavern that always makes me think about life. It's how I often feel – that I'm working my way through some underground network totally unable to see where I'm heading. I have no idea where I'm going, but I know that I have to keep moving. Perhaps I'm hoping, like the character in my story, that I'll stumble upon a magical exit that brings me out into the bright daylight. Instead it seems like an unending series of pitch black tunnels.

Maybe that's why (OK, I think that's definitely why) I found the story wanted to put another character into the cavern. Despite not knowing where I'm going to end up, I don't often feel like I'm alone. I can't see my hand in front of my face, let alone another person, but I know he's there. Sometimes it's like I'm just standing around, wondering where to go. Am I even facing the right direction? I don't know. Then I get a gentle push, or a voice whispering encouragement in my ear. Instead of jumping out of my skin (as I would in real life) I allow myself to get infected with hope. I'm not alone in here.

It's usually enough to keep me going for a while, gingerly pressing on, hoping that my passing might lift the darkness a little in the lives of others. Because I think that's really all God asks of any of us – just keep going.

The Wind and the Waves

04 October 2018

The wind and the waves crashed against the sides of the boat, so frail out there in the middle of the dark sea all by itself. Keeping steady footing was impossible, and keeping a steady head even harder.

And as the crew huddled together and screamed and wept and wished it were all a dream, The Man slept the sleep of the righteous, undisturbed and unafraid, the fury of nature powerless to break his peace.

"Don't you love us?" cried the crew to the sleeping figure. "Don't you care?"

The Man's eyes flicked open. He slowly sat, then stood, somehow not seeming to mind that the world was doing its best to toss him overboard.

"Do I love you?" he said to the trembling shadows huddled in the middle of the deck. "Do I care?"

The crew looked nervously at one another. This seemed like an inappropriate time for rhetorical questions.

"Be at peace," said The Man to the frightened crew, but it was the wind and the waves that heard. It was the wind and the waves that obeyed.

The churning black coil became a flawless crystal platter. The relentless angry howling disappeared into the silence. The stars twinkled mischievously in the endless charcoal, winking at the crew and saying, "And what exactly were you worried about?"

The world slept.

"Do I love you?" said The Man.

"Do I care?

"The wind and the waves shook me and screamed in my ear. I pushed them away because I was tired. But for you I woke.

"The wind and the waves were still and at peace when I spoke. They had to be. They had no choice. But to you I give the gift of disobedience.

"Do I love you?

"Do I care?"

The Man stretched his arms wide to encompass the whole of creation.

"You tell me."

A Week in the Life of

11 October 2018

On Monday God gave me some grace.

I squandered it on something. I don't even remember what it was now.

On Tuesday God gave me some grace.

I put it in a cupboard somewhere and forgot about it. It's probably still there.

On Wednesday God gave me some grace.

I told myself that it wasn't such a big deal if I went off somewhere and did whatever I wanted, because God would always turn up tomorrow with more grace.

On Thursday God gave me some grace.

God must think I'm pretty special. I enjoy feeling special.

On Friday God gave me some grace.

I sat back and relaxed, 'safe in the knowledge there'll always be a bit of my heart devoted to it,' as the song goes.

On Monday someone needed some grace.

But I was too busy, and I felt like I didn't have much to spare.

On Tuesday someone needed some grace.

But it was someone I didn't like very much, and I didn't really think that they deserved my grace.

On Wednesday someone needed some grace.

But I gave them some grace a couple of weeks ago! Couldn't they go somewhere else? Did they think I was made of grace?

On Thursday someone needed some grace.

But I didn't really trust them to use my grace wisely, so I gave it to someone who didn't really need it (but at least they probably wouldn't waste it).

On Friday someone needed some grace.

And I sat back and wondered why I felt like there was something not quite right with the world.

Cold-Calling

18 October 2018

I recently had a chat on my doorstep with two Jehovah's Witnesses (has anyone ever had a chat with a Jehovah's Witness that *wasn't* on a doorstep?). They were two perfectly nice friendly men with smiles that had only the vaguest hint of plasticness. There was a younger fellow (the Trainee) who asked most of the questions, and an older fellow (the Trainer) who interjected to steer the conversation back on track when I wasn't playing ball. Well, I say it was a 'conversation', but…

The list of questions they asked me read like an Alpha Course Greatest Hits compilation ("Does God Care?", "What About Suffering?", "What Do You Think About The Devil?") but it fell short of being an actual conversation. The whole thing quickly took on a surreal quality when I realised that my side of the exchange was totally irrelevant. It was like they were working through a predetermined cold-calling script, and the purpose of the questions was to move through a mental checklist and get on to the next listed query, with the eventual goal of…well, I don't know what the eventual goal was. I assume that it was the theological equivalent of getting me to admit that *yes, I had recently had an accident that wasn't my fault*. I honestly think that I could have responded to the question "Do you believe in God?" with "Squiggily diggily doo" and they wouldn't have even batted an eyelid, instead just ploughed on to ask me if I thought God cared about me (Spoiler: I said "Yes.").

Any attempt to divert the conversation into freeform territory was ignored. For example, when I challenged something they'd said, and suggested that the Bible was more concerned with the question of *how we should respond* to suffering rather than the question of why God allows it (Ask me about suffering will you? A subject I wrote my Master's thesis on? BIG MISTAKE.) it didn't even merit a response. The next thing I knew I was being offered a phone to read 1 John 5:19 and asked what I thought about the Devil. What? If I wanted to have my boundless wisdom and insightful commentary ignored I'd volunteer to do more preaching, thank you very much.

What I had wanted to do was ask *them* a question. Namely, what difference does your faith make to your lives? Not in a "Well, I'm spending my Saturday mornings knocking on people's doors" way, though that would be a fair response. Rather, how do you experience God in your life on a day-to-day basis? I would have been genuinely interested in their answers to that.

I didn't get the chance though. The Trainer cut the 'conversation' short. They'd just started hinting at some weird things about the Devil, and I guess he realised that he was five seconds away from getting a lecture on the evils of dualism. They did offer to come back sometime for a longer conversation, but I declined because my house is already full of people who ignore everything I say.

After we'd exchanged firm handshakes and goodbyes, I closed the door and began deconstructing what had just happened (honestly, my brain won't even give me five minutes to myself sometimes). I realised that this was the longest conversation I'd had with religious cold-callers in a while, possibly ever. Usually I'm super quick to dismiss them and send them away. I tell myself it's because it's futile to debate with people on the doorstep, a belief kind of borne out by what had just happened, but I also realised that this wasn't the whole truth. It's because every time I have an encounter like this I always come away feeling like I did a bad job and failed in some significant way. What do I expect from such events? A miracle conversion right there and then? Literally seeing the scales fall away from someone's eyes? When I think about it, it seems ridiculous, but if I'm honest there's a part of me that genuinely believes that anything less is a failure. As a result I'm quick to shut down what I regard as 'pointless' debates, mostly to protect myself from feeling that way. It's a bad habit that I need to keep an eye on.

Sometimes, in my interactions with other people, I learn more about myself than I do about them. I guess I owe those two Jehovah's Witnesses a debt of gratitude after all.

Three Years a Blogger

24 October 2018

Blogging is not rocket science (unless you're a rocket scientist who's blogging about rocket science), but even the simplest things can take their toll over a prolonged period. It's been three years now. Three years. Three years of tapping away each week on my keyboard and releasing something into the cyberwild. At times it feels like pitching rocks into a river on a dark night – there may be ripples, but there's no way of telling. Unless you can see in the dark – maybe with some kind of night vision goggles. I don't know, this simile is getting away from me.

At least I've learned stuff from the three years I've spent blogging. For example:

a) sometimes what I think is clever and funny writing, isn't.

b) the difference between 'learned' and 'learnt' (It turns out it's really just a stylistic choice, with 'learnt' being less common generally and practically unused in North America).

c) I actually have more to say than I thought I did, except when I don't nurture my relationship with God, and then it turns out that I actually have less to say than I thought I did.

So I just wanted to thank all of you who have engaged with my writing on some level, whether you've read any of my books or even if you're just an infrequent blog reader who keeps forgetting to unsubscribe. I am thankful for you.

And for that select few who occasionally write something in response to my ramblings, an extra big 'Thank You'.

Of course, there are a few people who, regardless of their commitment to the blog, deserve special gratitude for their long-suffering support of my endeavours. If you're thinking "I wonder if he's talking about me?" then I probably am.

I can't promise another three years, but let's see how we go, shall we?

About the Author

James is a writer, a father, a husband, a follower of Jesus and a lover of board games, though not necessarily in that order. Sometimes he even manages to do some of these things quite well. He's crammed quite a lot of experiences into his life so far, such as working for Tearfund; being a Baptist minister; living in Australia as part of a mission and discipleship community and watching Q.P.R. beat Oldham Athletic at Loftus Road on the 27th December 1993. It's not been all bad.

He and his family currently live in Canterbury, England.

Books by the Same Author

The Listening Book:
The Soul Painting & Other Stories

This is a beautiful book, in words and images, and will appeal to old and young and all those in between. As the title suggests, the stories are perfect for reading aloud and could be used in a range of settings. The delicate images add another dimension. From fables to folk tales, from stories told around the camp fire to John Lewis Christmas ads, humankind responds to the power of story and to the meaning that narratives give us.
Sophie Duffy
Author of *Bright Stars*, *The Generation Game* and *This Holey Life*.

Job 28 pictures the search for wisdom as digging for gold. The Listening Book has numerous nuggets to mine, embedded in stories that will help you to remember them.
Steve Divall
Senior Pastor, St Helen's Church, North Kensington.

Hardback ISBN: 978-0-9934383-0-1   Softback ISBN: 978-0-9934383-2-5
EBook ISBN: 978-0-9934383-1-8 Audiobook via Amazon/Audible
Religion: Inspirational
Lioness Writing Ltd Release date: 31 October 2015
144 pages, 8.5 inches x 8.5 inches, 25 colour photographs and 3 B&W photos

The Second Listening Book: Loaded Question & Other Stories

I enjoy reading James Webb, not just because he is a gifted and imaginative storyteller, but because he provides nourishing soul food for the journeys we all make through the deserts of life. With his creative imagination he provokes a range of emotions in the reader and I invite you to step inside and be prepared to find something for which your soul has cried out.
David Coffey OBE
Global Ambassador for BMS World Mission.

There are very few books I read that can make me laugh and think profoundly at the same time. This book however is one of them. As a child I used to watch Tales of the Unexpected and loved the twists at the end - James' book easily surpasses them. It is very easy to read and yet worthwhile at the same time as each story contains spiritual truths (which aren't at all preachy and sometimes not obvious!). This is a book you have to try - you won't regret it.
Eric Harmer
Pastor of Barton Church, Canterbury and Author of *Build-Your-Own Bible Study.*

Hardback ISBN: 978-0-9934383-6-3   Softback ISBN: 978-0-9934383-4-9
EBook ISBN: 978-0-9934383-7-0 Audiobook via Amazon/Audible
Religion: Inspirational
Lioness Writing Ltd Release date: 31 October 2016
158 pages, 8.5 inches x 8.5 inches, 31 black & white illustrations and photos

The Ramblings of the Man who Bought a Pear

James's Blog started in October 2015 and has become a weekly phenomenon that adds salt and light to the internet. This first year of posts is a rich collection of things in his head that he has been brave enough to release into the wild. 'The Man who Sold me a Pear' won the 2016 Association of Christian Writers 'Good Samaritan' short story award in partnership with Street Pastors.
www.thelisteningbook.org.uk

The Association of Christian Writers is a fellowship of writers sharing prayerful support and encouragement as well as giving professional standards of training and advice. They support Christian writers overseas, in the developing world and Eastern Europe. www.christianwriters.org.uk

Street Pastors are trained volunteers from local churches who serve their community during the small hours of the weekend. Teams of men and women patrol from 10 pm to 4 am on a Friday and Saturday night, to care for, listen to and help people who are out on the streets. Proceeds from this book will help support this work. www.streetpastors.org

Comments on 'The Man who Sold me a Pear':
Anne: I had a tear in my eye too!
Jon: Can really relate to this one. Thanks for writing it.
David: I just discovered your Blog. Love it and the honesty in sharing your life and faith. This story about buying a pear really touched me. Cheers James.

Softback £5.99/$10 ISBN: 978-0-9934383-8-7
Religion: Inspirational
Published by Lioness Writing Ltd, Member of CSPA
<lionesswritingltd@gmail.com>
Release date: 31 October 2016
170 pages
8 inches x 5 inches

The Ramblings of the Man who Likes to Eat Alone

James's Blog then carried on for a second year. So that is what is in this book.

Softback £5.99/$10 ISBN: 978-1-9997464-1-4
Religion: Inspirational
Published by Lioness Writing Ltd,
Member of CSPA <lionesswritingltd@gmail.com>
Release date: 30 November 2017
148 pages
8 inches x 5 inches

More Posts

www.thelisteningbook.org.uk

You can contact James at

author@thelisteningbook.org.uk

www.ingramcontent.com/pod-product-compliance
Lightning Source LLC
Chambersburg PA
CBHW030523080526
44586CB00011B/302